RE:ZERO -STARTING LIFE IN ANOTHER WORLD-

Chapter 3: Truth of Zero

INTRODUCTION TO THE MAIN CAST

"I'LL SAVE YOU—I SWEAR!"

SUBARU NATSUKI

"SHEESH... YOU'RE SUCH A POTATO-HEAD."

EMILIA

A beautiful girl with silver hair an violet eyes Subaru met in the capital Has a benevolent, caring personalit but won't own up to it for som reason. Only opens up before Puck her cat spirit companion, who's a close as family. Encountered Subar when searching for an object an took the gradually unreliable Subar on the same path as herself.

"SISTER IS INCREDIBLE."

REM

Younger of the twin maids at the mansion where Subaru is carried to after a noble sacrifice. Master of all things domestic, with her own backhanded barbed tongue. She carries essentially the entire mansion on her shoulders. Calm in appearance and gently sarcastic, she rarely shows even a slight smile except to her beloved older sister.

"I'LL HAVE YOU KNOW, STEAMED POTATOES ARE RAM'S SPECIALTY."

RAM

Elder of the twin maids at Roswa Manor, where the injured Subaru wa brought. Arrogant, with a barbe tongue. Inferior to her younge sister in cooking, cleaning, sewing and laundry. Sharp-eyed, sharp i demeanor, and very strict in he training regimen.

"WHAT DO YOU DESIRE?"

ROSWAAL

A noble of the Kingdom of Lugunica and a marquis with substantial power. One of the kingdom's foremost magic users, he is known as the "Court Magician" at the palace. An eccentric putting his lofty title to waste with his bizarre words, actions, and makeup. Apparently dyes his face white and acts like a clown before others because he prefers it.

"EVERYTHING IN THIS WORLD IS TO MY CONVENIENCE!"

PRISCILLA BARIEL

A beautiful girl Subaru saved whe she was surrounded by thugs in th capital. Arrogant in attitude, bol and dramatic in conduct, she walk a self-centered path to greatness Known as "The Bloody Bride," she i one candidate for the next Queen o Lugunica.

"SWEET UPPERCUT THERE, NICE ONE, PRINCESS."

AL

One-armed man wearing a thick iron helm and bandit-chic clothes below the neck. Has a stout physique and feels like a seasoned veteran but stands out due to his casual, frivolous demeanor. His appearance and speaking style made him Priscilla's knight more than his combat ability. He was summoned to the other world, just like Subaru.

"I'M BUSY. LIVE LIFE TO THE FULLEST!"

FELT

A street urchin with dirty blond hai and unyielding red eyes. Her fan is especially charming. Raised i the capital's slums, she has a toug persona belying her age. Live mainly as a pickpocket, but th glowing badge in her hand turne her into a candidate for the throne.

REINHARD

A handsome young man with fiery red hair and sky blue eyes. His every word and action is filled with a superhuman level of consideration for others. Known as the "Sword Saint" and "Knight of Knights," he is famous throughout the capital.

"CUT IT OUT ALREADY! WHAT ARE YOU TRYING TO DO, BREAK THE DOOR DOWN BECAUSE YOU DON'T KNOW THE PASSWORD!?"

OLD MAN ROM

An elderly giant boasting a fram over two meters in height. The fac of a building known as the loot cella in the capital's slums. In contrast t his stern appearance, he takes goo care of others, sometimes too muc for their liking.

NOW, THEN ...
THE NEXT CANDI-DATE, EMILIA !!
Y-YES ...!
A SILVER-HAIRED HALF-ELF.
A HALF-DEMON!? HOW FILTHY!

IT'S ALL RIGHT, SUBARU. BELIEVE IN LADY EMILIA...

HEY, DON'T GO READING MY MIND! AM I THAT OBVIOUS!?

THAT'S RIGHT! I HAVE TO BELIEVE IN HER...

EMILIA'S BEEN WORKING BEHIND THE SCENES ALL ALONG.
I KNOW THAT ALL TOO WELL!

MURMUR...
MURMUR...

ZA (STEP)

MYYY, TO COME AFTER ALL THESE KNIGHTS...
...I FEEL SO TEEERRIBLY OUT OF PLACE.
YES?
......
SHE'S COMPLETELY SHRINKING IN THE FACE OF THEIR ILL WILL...
LADY EMILIA AND MARQUIS ROSWAAL L. MATHERS!
PLEASE ADDRESS THE CHAMBER!!

G-GREETINGS TO ALL ASSEMBLED...! M-MY NAME IS...E-EMILIA...
I HAVE NO FAMILY NAME...
P-PLEASE SIMPLY CALL ME EMILIA...

TH...
THIS IS BAD!!

ROSWAAAL!!

DO YOU UNDER-STAND!?
JUST HAVING THIS SILVER-HAIRED HALF-DEMON ENTER THE THRONE ROOM DEFILES IT!!

ギリ
GIRI (CLENCH)

MR. BORDEAUX, YOUR WORDS GO TOO FAR.
SURELY YOU UNDER-STAND, MR. MIKLOTOV !!

IS SHE NOT THE SPITTING IMAGE OF THE WITCH OF JEALOUSY...
...THE HALF-DEMON WHO SWALLOWED AND DESTROYED HALF THE WORLD IN THE OLD TALES!?

HOW MUCH DO YOU THINK THE MERE SIGHT OF HER MAKES US TREMBLE!?

IT SEEMS THAT YOU UNDERSTAND PERFECTLY WELL, LORD BORDEAUX.

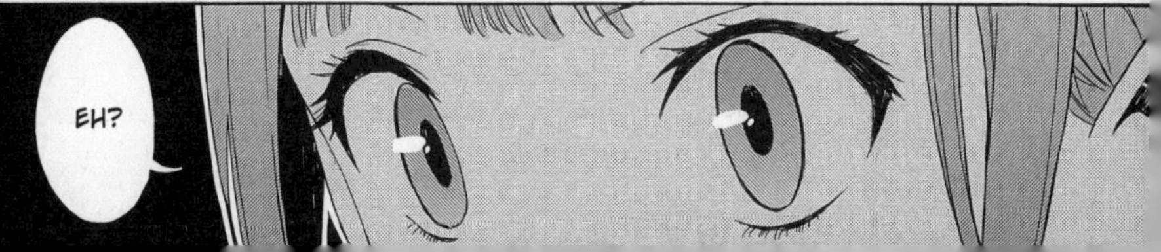
EH?

WHAT DO YOU MEAN, ROSWAAL!?

AS YOU HAVE SAID, IT WILL BE DIFFICULT FOR THE POPULACE TO ACCEPT HER.
HOWEVER, THAT MAKES HER A VALUABLE PIECE UPON OUR CHESSBOARD.

PERHAPS IT IS A POOOOR CHOICE OF WORDING, BUT...
...WOULD YOU THINK OF HER AS A SACRIFICIAL PAWN?
IN OTHER WORDS...

...THE ROYAL SELECTION IS, IN FACT, A FOUR-PERSON CONTEST...
PRECISELY ...
... LORD MIKLO-TOV.

DON'T GIVE ME...
ROSWAAL!

...THAT CRAP!
SUBARU!!
EVEN I DID NOT THINK YOU WOULD FAIL TO REALIZE YOUR STATION.

BEHOLD FIRE MANA OF THE GREATEST POWER—
BO (WHOOSH)
GOU (ROAR)
ALGOA!!

DO (WHAM)
OOO (SSSS)
GOOD-NESS...

YOU REALLY ARE RUNNING YOUR MOUTHS...
...IN FRONT OF MY DAUGHTER, YOU LOWLY HUMANS.
DON (BAM)
PUCK!!
FWISH
THAT IS ENOUGH. I SHALL PERMIT NO FURTHER VIOLENCE IN MY PRESENCE...

IF YOU CONTINUE—
THEN I'M PREPARED TO WIELD MY POWER ...
...AS MY BELOVED DAUGHTER DEMANDS!

THE APOC-ALYPSE BEAST...
...OF ETERNAL FROST...!?
AH, RIGHT. SOME HAVE CALLED ME THAT.
SEEMS YOU'RE INFORMED FOR A YOUNGIN.

AS YOU SURMISE, LORD MIKLOTOV...
...THIS SUPERNATURAL BEING IS A GREAT SPIRIT OF YORE KNOWN AS "THE APOCALYPSE BEAST"...

...AND AT PRESENT, IS LADY EMILIA'S CONTRACTED SPIRIT.

ABSURD...! ONE OF THE FOUR GREAT SPIRITS WOULD NEVER SERVE A—

YOU SHOULD BE GRATEFUL TO LIA...
GOO (SURGE)

IT'S ONLY THANKS TO MY ADORABLE, BELOVED DAUGHTER'S PLEAS...
...THAT I HAVE NOT TURNED YOU INTO ICICLES ON THE SPOT.
GOGOGOGO (RUMBLE)
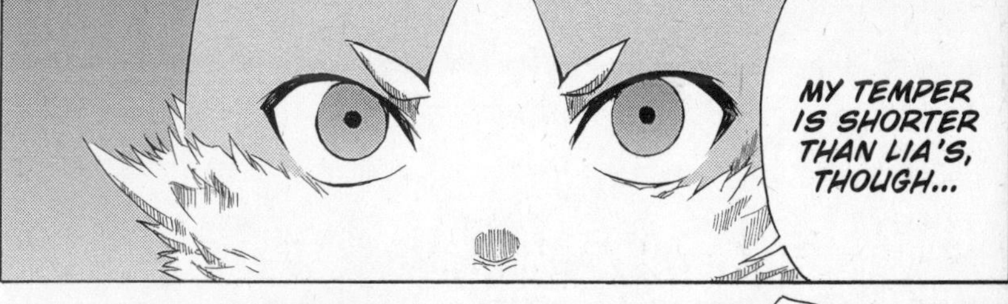
MY TEMPER IS SHORTER THAN LIA'S, THOUGH...

...!!

HO HO HO...

AN AMUSING, HEART-STIRRING PLOY, MR. ROSWAAL...

SO THE GAME IS UP.
AS EXPECTED OF LORD MIKLOTOV...
EH...?

THIS HAS ALL BEEN AN ACT TO...
...DEMONSTRATE THE GREAT SPIRIT'S POWER TO US AND...
...INDICATE THAT LADY EMILIA WIELDS CONSID-ERABLE POWER.
I KNEW IT...
IT'S NOT GOOD TO OVERDO IT, ROSWAAL!
I WAS SO SURE OF IT, THOUGH...
EH!?
EHH!?
AND I TOTALLY FELL FOR IT...
ROSWAAL!!
DO YOU EVEN APPRE-CIATE...
...WHAT YOU HAVE DONE HERE!!?

I APOLOGIZE, LORD BORDEAUX.

BUT WE WOULD NOT EVEN BE HAVING THIS CONVERSA-TION...
...WERE IT NOT FOR LADY EMILIA'S WARMTH AND KINDNESS...

IS THAT A THREAT, ROSWAAL!?

THAT'S RIGHT...
...I AM THREAT-ENING YOU.

LIA...?
I'M SORRY...
PUCK, ROSWAAL...

I'M ALL RIGHT NOW.

ALLOW ME TO...
...MAKE MY CASE ONCE MORE TO THE ESTEEMED COUNCIL OF ELDERS.

MY NAME IS EMILIA.

I HAVE NO FAMILY NAME.
CALL ME EMILIA—NOTHING MORE.
YES...
...I AM THREATENING YOU.
I HAVE BUT A SINGLE DEMAND.

—FAIR TREATMENT!
FAIR TREATMENT IS EXCEEDINGLY VALUABLE TO ME.

THAT IS WHY I WILL NOT BREATHE ONE WORD ABOUT USING MY...
...CONTRACTED SPIRIT AS A SHIELD TO UNFAIRLY SEIZE THE THRONE!
I AM INEXPERIENCED IN EVERY WAY COMPARED TO THE OTHER CANDIDATES.
THERE IS MUCH I DO NOT KNOW...

...AND A MOUNTAIN OF THINGS I MUST LEARN.
HENCE, I WILL CONTINUE TO STRIVE.

FOR HERE, TODAY...
...I KNOW THE SUMMIT I MUST REACH...!
I DO NOT KNOW IF MY EFFORTS ARE WORTHY OF THE THRONE...
...BUT NONE OF THE OTHER CANDIDATES' FEELINGS RUN DEEPER THAN MINE!

I HAVE NO FAMILY NAME. I AM SIMPLY EMILIA.
THEREFORE, PLEASE LOOK AT ME WITH FAIR EYES.

LADY EMILIA...

...MY OPINION SHALL NOT CHANGE.

WHEN CONSIDERING THE EFFECTS OF YOUR APPEARANCE ON THE PEOPLE...
...YOUR TENUOUS POSITION IN THIS ROYAL SELECTION IS UNCHANGED...!

—HOW-EVER...

...I DO APOLOGIZE FOR MY EARLIER RUDENESS...
...LADY EMILIA!

THOUGH THAT WAS A RATHER STORMY DIGRESSION ...
...DO YOU HAVE NO MORE WORDS?
NO...
...I DO NOT!

—THEN, LADY EMILIA, LORD ROSWAAL ...
... THANK YOU VERY MUCH!!

INCIDEN-TALLY, LADY EMILIA.

WHAT IS THIS INDIVIDUAL'S POSITION?

HE IS, AH... ...ERR...

IT'S ALL RIGHT, EMILIA!
I'M READY FOR THIS TOO.
EH!?
WAIT A MINUTE, SUBARU!
SORRY FOR THE LATE GREETING!
LORDS OF THE COUNCIL OF ELDERS!
MY NAME IS SUBARU NATSUKI!
A SERVANT AT ROSWAAL MANOR AND...

BI (POINT)
...LADY EMILIA'S ...
... KNIGHT !!

Re:ZERO -Starting Life in Another World-

Truth of Zero

The only ability Subaru Natsuki gets when he's summoned to another world is time travel via his own death. But to save her, he'll die as many times as it takes.

The only ability Subaru Natsuki gets when he's summoned to another world is time travel via his own death. But to save her, he'll die as many times as it takes.

Truth of Zero

Re:ZERO -Starting Life in Another W

MY NAME IS SUBARU NATSUKI.
A SERVANT AT ROSWAAL MANOR AND...

Episode 7 Subaru Natsuki, the Self-Proclaimed Knight

Episode 7 Subaru Natsuki, the Self-Proclaimed Knight
Re:ZERO -Starting Life in Another World-
Truth of Zero
[PRISCILLA BARIEL]
● One of the candidates to succeed Lugunica's king.
● Subaru saved Priscilla from peril when they met, but she feels no debt to him.
● Bold, dramatic, and highly confident. Fond of saying "This world is solely for my convenience."
● Bewitching men with her captivating beauty, she has married seven men in the past, but each partner died within a year. She is known as "The Bloody Bride."
● Despises tedium and loves tumult. She apparently made Al her knight because he was the oddest one available.
● Possesses extraordinary genius, succeeding at whatever she does, but rarely does anything herself.
● Special skills: [Aesthetic Eye], [Dragon Rider], [Sword Dance]
● Hobbies: [Reading], [Theater], [Artistic Appraisal]

......

ER...?
THAT'S NOT THE REACTION I EXPECTED...

HMM...A KNIGHT, ARE YOU...

MARQUIS ROSWAAL... COULD YOU EXPLAIN?

THE BOY IS SOMEWHAT IGNORANT OF HIS PLAAACE.

THEN, DOES...
...LADY EMILIA ACTUALLY HAVE A KNIGHT?

ABOOOUT THAT...

UNLIKE THE OTHER CANDI-DATES...
...LADY EMILIA CURRENTLY LACKS A KNIGHT SHE CAN TRUST.
HOOOWEVER, THAT DOES NOT MEAN AAANYONE CAN TAKE UP THE POST...

...PARTICULARLY ONE CALLING HIMSELF A KNIGHT FOR SOMEONE WHO...
...MIGHT WELL BECOME QUEEN.

THE QUALIFICATIONS TO BE A KNIGHT ARE...

...FIDELITY TOWARD ONE'S MASTER...
...THE STRENGTH TO PROTECT ONE'S LIEGE...
...AND SOMETHING SPECIAL ENABLING ONE TO BLAZE A PAAATH FOR THE MASTER WHO...
...IS TO BECOME MONARCH.

THAT ALONE IS NOT ENOUGH, MARQUIS ROSWAAL.
HE IS LACKING IN CAPACITY.
WHAT DID YOU SAY...!?

NOTHING IS GAINED BY ATTEMPTING TO SURPASS ONE'S CAPACITY.
THAT ALSO APPLIES TO THE TITLE OF "KNIGHT."

THAT'S... NOT SOME-THING YOU KNOW UNLESS YOU TRY!!

I DO.

WE KNIGHTS TRAIN IN BODY AND SPIRIT DAY AFTER DAY...
...IN FULL AWARENESS OF FACT.
IS YOUR RESOLVE EQUAL TO THEIRS?

RESOLVE ISN'T SO HIGH AND MIGHTY...

I'LL MAKE EMILIA THE QUEEN!
I'LL MAKE HER WISH COME TRUE!

DO YOU NOT THINK THAT REPLY ARROGANT?
CLAIMING YOU POSSESS THE POWER TO DO THIS...?

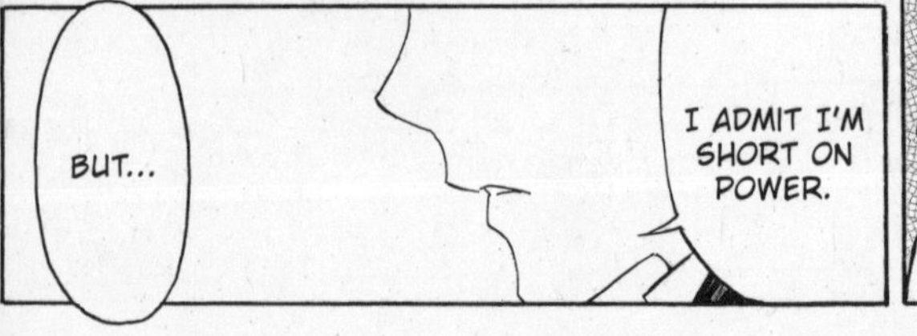
I ADMIT I'M SHORT ON POWER.
BUT...

...THAT DOESN'T CHANGE MY ANSWER!
MY FEELINGS ARE NO LESS VALID THAN SOMEONE TALKING...
...TO PUT HIMSELF AND HIS PALS ON A PEDESTAL!!
FEELINGS... YOU SAY?

DO YOU THINK YOUR FEELINGS STRONGER AND PURER THAN...
...THOSE HERE WHO HAVE WORKED FOR THEIR QUALIFICATIONS?
SPITTING OUT BLOOD IN THEIR DRIVE TO ALWAYS BE THE BEST...
...READY TO THROW THEIR LIVES AWAY FOR THE GREATNESS STANDING BEHIND THEM...
...THAT IS WHAT PRECEDES THE HONOR OF QUALIFYING TO BE A KNIGHT!

—EVEN SO...
...I'LL MAKE EMILIA QUEEN.
I DO NOT UNDER-STAND.
WHY DO YOU CONTINUE TO STAND HERE AND DENY IT SO?
—BECAUSE SHE'S SPECIAL.

FINE, THEN...
I UNDERSTAND YOU ARE DETERMINED TO PROTECT WHAT IS IMPORTANT TO YOU.
I HAVE NO MORE WORDS FOR YOU.
YOU ARE OBSTINATE.
—HOWEVER, I INDEED CANNOT ACKNOWLEDGE YOU AS A "KNIGHT."
A KNIGHT WOULD NEVER CAUSE...
...THE ONE HE HOPES TO STAND BY TO WEAR SUCH AN EXPRESSION.
ZA (STEP)

THAT'S... ENOUGH...
... SUBARU ...

LORDS OF THE COUNCIL OF ELDERS...
...I APOLOGIZE FOR THIS WASTE OF YOUR TIME.

HE SHALL WITHDRAW IMMEDIATELY.

I WOULD CALL THE TIME WELL SPENT, LADY EMILIA.
HE HAS SHOWN TO ONE AND ALL THAT YOU ARE NOT A...
...HALF-ELF THE WORLD SHOULD FEAR.

YOU HAVE A FINE VASSAL.

SUBARU IS NO VASSAL OF MINE.

TAKE A BREATHER OUTSIDE FOR A WHILE, ALL RIGHT?

AT THAT RATE, I'D HAVE JUST CAUSED HER MORE TROUBLE ...
NO, NOT THAT ...

I COULDN'T HAVE TAKEN ANY MORE OF...
...THAT COLD LOOK FROM EMILIA...!

SORRY! LET US PASS! WE'VE CAUGHT AN INTRUDER!
IT'LL WAIT! THE CONFERENCE IS UNDERWAY JUST AHEAD!!

THERE ARE REASONS THIS CAN'T WAIT!
WE NEED ORDERS FROM THE CAPTAIN!

—OLD MAN ROM!?

DON'T TELL ME HE FOLLOWED ME HERE!?

WHAT IS IT? DO YOU KNOW THIS INTRUDER ...?
ER, AH...
THAT'S ...
HMPH ...

IS A FILTHY OLD MAN THAT RARE A SIGHT!?
THAT'S A NOBLEMAN'S TASTES FOR YA!
YOU!! WATCH YOUR MOUTH!!
OLD MAN ROM'S...
...COVERING FOR ME...
FELT'S UP AHEAD, AIN'T SHE?
EH?
MNN!!
GO (SLAM)
WHY, YOU!!

GA (WHAM)
RRGH!!
WHOA ...!?
DO (THUD)
OLD MAN ROM !?
WAIT FOR ME...
...FELT!

YOU DRAGGED ME HERE FROM THE SLUMS AGAINST MY WILL!!
I NEVER HAD ANY INTENTION OF BECOMING QUEEN!

SHE WAS BORN IN THE SLUMS ...!?
WHAT WAS REINHARD THINKING ...!?
I UNDER-STAND ALL OF YOUR CONCERNS ...
LADY FELT WAS RAISED IN THE SLUMS UNTIL ABOUT A MONTH AGO.
BY PURE CHANCE, I CAME TO...
...LEARN THAT SHE IS QUALIFIED TO BE A DRAGON MAIDEN.

I SENSED THAT THIS "COINCIDENCE" WAS FATE!
SHE IS WORTHY OF BEING THE NEXT QUEEN...!

HEY, YOU!! DID YOU LISTEN TO A WORD I SAID!?

WHO GOES THERE!?
WHY, YOU...
AHH...!?

WHAT?

BAN (SLAM)

OLD MAN ROM ...!?
...FELT!

NOW!! SEIZE HIM!!
UGH...

OLD MAN ROM!!
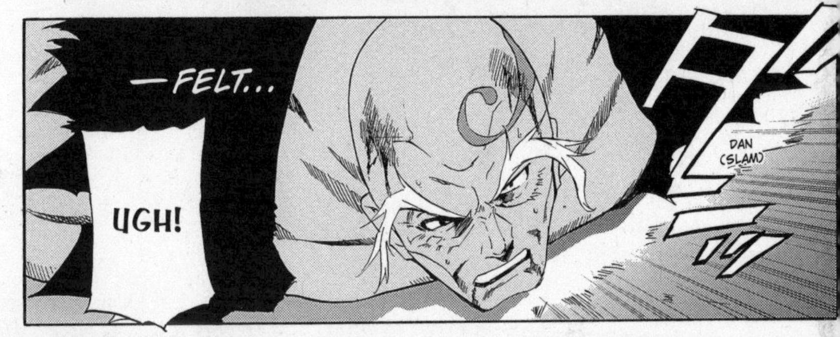
DAN (SLAM)
—FELT...
UGH!

STOP IT!! LET HIM GO!
NO NEED TO WORRY ABOUT ME...
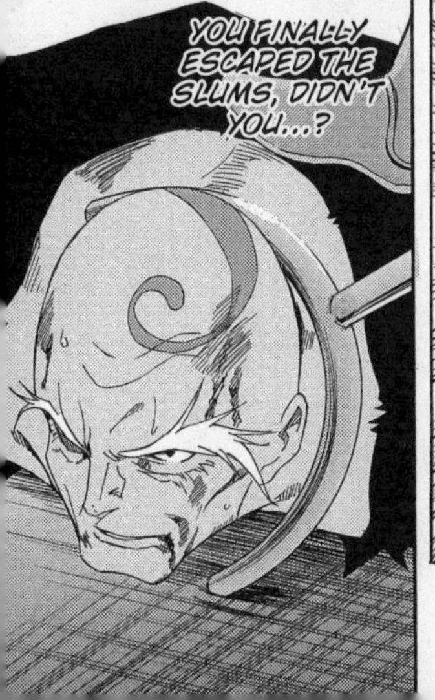
YOU FINALLY ESCAPED THE SLUMS, DIDN'T YOU...?

HEY, YOU!! TELL THEM TO LET OLD MAN ROM GO!!
HE ONLY CAME HERE BECAUSE HE WAS WORRIED ABOUT ME!!

UNFORTUNATELY, I CANNOT COMPLY.

AS YOU STATED PREVIOUSLY, YOU HAVE NO INTENTION OF JOINING THE ROYAL SELECTION.
IF YOU WILL NOT ACCEPT OUR SWORDS, YOU ARE NOT QUALIFIED TO ISSUE ORDERS TO US.

AH, IS THAT SO?

TO (TOK)
LADY FELT.

STOP IT!! FELT, STAY OUT OF THIS!!
DON'T WORRY ABOUT ME!!

DIDN'T YOU ALWAYS WANT TO GET OUT OF LIFE IN THE SLUMS!?
YOUR HAPPINESS IS IN THIS WORLD!!

—GEEZ, NOT YOU TOO...

ビリッ
BIRI (RIP)
EVERY LAST ONE OF YOU...
...PUSHING YOUR RIDICULOUS IDEAS ONTO ME!!

SURE, I ALWAYS WANTED TO GET OUT OF THE SLUMS...
I HATED THAT DUMP.
BUT...
HOW CAN I BE HAPPY WHILE I...
...TURN MY BACK ON MY OWN FAMILY!?

FELT...
I'LL SAY IT AGAIN...
LET HIM GO...
OLD MAN ROM IS FAMILY TO ME.
AS THE CAPTAIN STATED, WE CANNOT OBEY A PRIVATE—
I'LL DO IT.

I'LL DO IT. THE ROYAL SELECTION THING.
I'LL AIM TO BE QUEEN TOO!
SO LET OLD MAN ROM GO— NOW.
AS YOU COM-MAND !!

FELT...
REINHARD!!
YES!
HERE!
ZA (ZIP)
GET HIS SHACKLES OFF.
THE SWORD SAINT?

RIGHT AWAY!
HYU (SWISH)

BARE-HANDED!?
YES.
PAKI (SNAP)
OHH...

SO THIS ALL...
...WENT THE WAY YOU WANTED?
NOT AT ALL.
THIS WAS GUIDED BY THE HAND OF FATE.

HAH! FATE AGAIN?
ARE YOU FATE'S SLAVE?
—NO.

I AM YOUR KNIGHT.

—I'LL BOSS YOU AROUND.
PLEASE BE GENTLE.

YEAH.
YOU CAN!

LADY FELT, SIR REINHARD.
MAY I TAKE THIS TO MEAN YOU ARE BOTH JOINING THE ROYAL SELECTION?

AS LONG AS IT IS MY MASTER'S WILL.

UNDER-STOOD.
—IT HAS BEEN SOMEWHAT TURBULENT...
...BUT ALL OF THE CANDIDATES ARE NOW ASSEMBLED.
ギィ
GII (CREAK)

—I HEREBY MOVE THAT THIS ROYAL SELECTION...
...MAY COMMENCE.
—IN THE NAME OF THE COUNCIL OF ELDERS, I SECOND.
AND I...
AND I...

—WELL, THEN...
LADY CRUSCH KARSTEN!
LADY PRISCILLA BARIEL!

LADY ANASTASIA HOSHIN!

LADY EMILIA!
LADY FELT!

EACH OF THESE FIVE...
...IS QUALIFIED TO BE A DRAGON MAIDEN.

THE ROYAL SELECTION IS THE COLLECTIVE WILL OF THE PEOPLE...

...AND HELD ACCORDING TO THE GUIDANCE OF THE DRAGON AND THE RADIANCE OF THE DRAGON JEWELS!

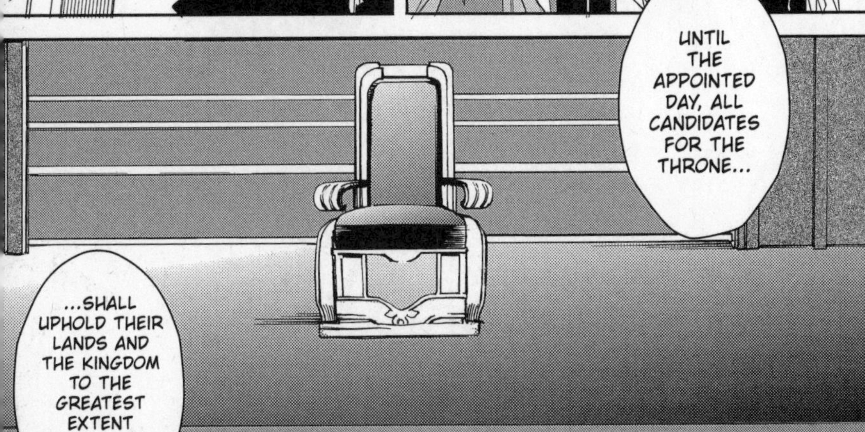
UNTIL THE APPOINTED DAY, ALL CANDIDATES FOR THE THRONE...
...SHALL UPHOLD THEIR LANDS AND THE KINGDOM TO THE GREATEST EXTENT POSSIBLE!

LET THE ROYAL SELEC-TION...
OOOOOOO (ROAR)
...COMMENCE!!

Episode 8 The Self-Declared Knight and the Knight Proper

Re:ZERO -Starting Life in Another World-

Truth of Zero

[CRUSCH KARSTEN]

- One of the candidates for the next Queen of Lugunica.
- Remarkable both as a beautiful woman in male attire and a duchess of the Kingdom of Lugunica.
- Counted old acquaintances among the now-deceased royal family so has a special regard for the empty throne. A royal selection candidate with great resolve and the undisputed favorite.
- A forthright, invigorating individual, with strict, stern beliefs, applied to both herself and others. Her skill with the sword has some calling her "Valkyrie."
- Has known her knight, Ferris, from a young age. The straitlaced Crusch and mischievous Ferris look like a pair of close sisters to others.
- A brilliant, hard worker who tends to focus on one thing at a time.
- Special skills: [Swordsmanship], [Dragon Riding], [Negotiation], [Cooking]
- Hobbies: [Swordsmanship], [Dragon Riding], [Playing Around with Ferris]

SUBARU!

REIN-
HARD!
FERRIS
!!

—IS THE CONFERENCE DONE ALREADY?

YES...
THE CANDIDATES HAVE REMAINED TO DISCUSS THE FINER DETAILS.

—ALSO, THAT OLD MAN IS SAFE AND SOUND.
!

LADY FELT INTERVENED TO ENSURE HIS SAFETY.
I GUESSED HE PASSED YOU ON THE WAY AND YOU MIGHT BE CONCERNED.

THAT SO...?
THANK GOODNESS.

WELL, IT'S JUST AS I FIGURED!
BETTER TO LEAVE IT TO YOU GUYS IN THE THRONE ROOM THAN FOR ME TO STUMBLE AROUND.

GLAD TO HAVE YOU CHECK UP ON ME, BUT...
...IS IT OKAY FOR YOU NOT TO BE AT YOUR MASTERS' SIDES?
THAT'S QUITE ALL RIGHT!

LADY CRUSCH IS A LOT STRONGER THAN FERRI ANYWAY!

HEY, NOW.
DON'T YOU KNIGHTS OF THE ROYAL GUARD HAVE TO BE STRONG?
FERRI HAS OTHER SELLING POINTS, MEOW.

YOU KNOW THAT, DON'T YOU, MEOW...
PITO (TOUCH)
... SUBA-WU?
R-RIGHT. HEARD YOU WERE INCREDIBLE WITH WATER MAGIC...
...!
YEAH, I FEEL LIKE ALL MY FATIGUE JUST LEFT MY BODY...

"INCRED-IBLE" DOESN'T QUITE COVER IT, SUBARU.
FERRIS HAS BEEN GRANTED THE TITLE OF "BLUE," THE PINNACLE OF THE ELEMENT.
AREN'T YOU LUCKY, SUBAWU?
YOU REALLY SHOULD THANK LADY EMILIA ...
...FOR HAVING FERRI TREATING YOU, HUH!

DO I NEED TO ACCEPT THAT TREATMENT?

COMPENSATION HAS ALREADY BEEN PAID, SO...
...IT'D MEAN PUTTING LADY EMILIA'S EFFORTS TO WASTE.

COMPENSATION ...?
CAN'T YOU JUST HAND THAT BACK?

UNFORTUNATELY, IT'S NOT SOMETHING PHYSICAL...
...BUT THE SORT OF THING THAT, ONCE YOU KNOW OF IT, YOU CAN'T GIVE BACK.

SHIT...! I'M JUST CAUSING HER TROUBLE NO MATTER WHAT I DO...

IF YOU LAMENT YOUR OWN POWERLESSNESS ...
...I BELIEVE THAT LEAVES YOU WITH A SINGLE, PROPER CHOICE.

YOU !?
WHAT ARE YOU DOING HERE !?
JULIUS...
SUBARU NATSUKI... I HAVE BUSINESS WITH YOU.
COME TO THE TRAINING GROUND.

JULIUS... YOU SHOULD STOP. THIS ISN'T LIKE YOU.

NORMALLY, I WOULD REFRAIN, REINHARD, MY FRIEND...
...BUT IN THIS CASE, THIS MAN'S STATEMENTS BELITTLED THE PATH OF CHIVALRY.

THAT IS HOW EVERY LAST PERSON HERE FEELS.

SUBARU NATSUKI ...
...YOU COULD HAVE BEEN CUT DOWN FOR YOUR INSOLENCE.

BUT, HOWEVER UNWITTINGLY, YOU ARE EMILIA'S VASSAL...
...SO LET US SETTLE THIS WITH WOODEN SWORDS...
PROVE YOURSELF TO ME.
CHA (RATTLE)
NOT WITH WORDS BUT WITH...
...THE SWORD!

ODDS ARE A HUNDRED TO ZERO.
DOESN'T FEEL LIKE ANYONE'S BETTING ON ME.
BUT...!
GA (GRAB)

DON'T UNDER-ESTIMATE HOW BAD I AM AT READING THE MOOD!!
SNAP

I AM PLEASED BY YOUR ENTHUSIASM ...!
FERRIS, REFEREE!
SURE!
BA (SUDDEN)
GOOD LUCK, SUBAWU.

AS LONG AS YOU DON'T DIE, I'LL HANDLE IT.

WHY SAY THAT ONLY TO ME!?
WORRY ABOUT THE OTHER GUY TOO!
HMPH...
I AM GRATEFUL FOR YOUR CONCERN.

SO, STARTING NOW...
...SUBARU NATSUKI AND JULIUS JUUKULIUS SHALL ENGAGE IN MOCK COMBAT!!
MAY BOTH DO THEIR UTMOST!!

KON (KNOCK)
KON
GACHA (RATTLE)
PARDON ME!
I MUST REPORT!
PRESENTLY, AT THE TRAINING GROUND, SIR JULIUS...
...AND LADY EMILIA'S RETAINER, SUBARU NATSUKI, ARE ENGAGED IN MOCK COMBAT!

SUBARU IS...?
WHY REPORT ABOUT MERE MOCK COMBAT?
YOU CAN DEAL WITH IT!
YES, WELL ...

IT IS SO UTTERLY ONE-SIDED...
...IT WAS THOUGHT BEST TO SEEK INSTRUCTIONS—

I'LL STOP THIS. SHOW ME THE WAY!
R-RIGHT AWAY!!
WHY...!? SUBARU...

HAA...
HAA...

WILL YOU FINALLY ACKNOWLEDGE YOUR INFERIORITY?
ANY FURTHER, AND I BELIEVE YOUR LIFE MIGHT BE IN JEOPARDY...

RELAX...I WON'T DIE FROM THIS MUCH.

YOU SPEAK AS IF YOU HAVE EXPERIENCE.

YEAH, I'M SOMETHING OF AN EXPERT ON THAT...

RAAH!!
CLUMSY, PREDICTABLE ATTACKS.
NO BEAUTY IN THEM...

GA (SMACK)
DOSHA (FLOP)

HAA!
HAA!
OW.
OW.
OW...
OW.
OW.
GAKH!
THIS IS... MY LAST CHANCE!
PROBABLY CAN'T GET BACK UP NEXT TIME...

...I HATE TO ADMIT IT, BUT I CAN'T BEAT HIM AS I AM NOW.
...EVEN SO...

...I'LL JUST GET ONE SHOT IN!!

JUST ONE LITTLE OPENING ...!
WAIT FOR IT...!

BAN (BURST)

SUBARU!!
AAARGH!
HE SEIZED AN OPENING!?
—BUT STILL TOO SLOW. THIS ENDS HERE.

SHAMAK!!
ZU
(BLOT)
!?
"DARK" MAGIC!?

GOTCHA!!
SO THIS IS YOUR TRUMP CARD.

BERI
(TEAR)

KA (FLASH)
POTA (DRIP)

ドッ
DO
(FLOP)

I ADMIT, YOU DID SURPRISE ME...
...BUT YOUR SKILL IN MAGIC IS FAR TOO LOW.
IT WOULD NOT HAVE WORKED UPON A SINGLE KNIGHT OF THE ROYAL GUARD...

SUBARU NATSUKI.
YOU... ARE POWER-LESS.
—I'M...
...POWER-LESS.

Episode 9
Alone

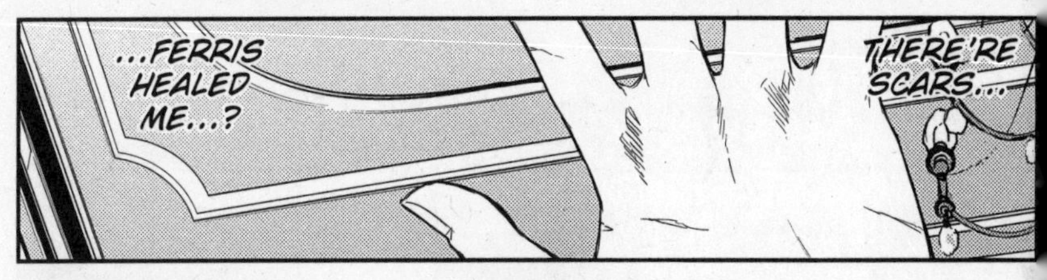

IT SEEMS YOU'RE AWAKE.

EMILIA...

SUBARU...

...LET'S TALK.

[ANASTASIA HOSHIN]
● One of the candidates to be the next Queen of Lugunica.
● Born in the neighboring nation's City-state of Kararagi, she is the young president of the Hoshin Company.
● Speaks the so-called "Kararagi Dialect" unique to that nation, but it sounds like Kansai Dialect any way you slice it.
● A small-statured, lovely girl, but she is the oldest of the candidates (save one exception). She craves the throne of a kingdom all her own, using her well-honed business acumen to pursue it.
● Extremely partial to fur, with much affection for the numerous beast-people under her command.
● A brilliant, hard worker who tends to focus on one thing at a time.
● Possesses overwhelming talent in a single field. "Merchant" is truly her ideal profession.
● Special skills: [Mathematical Calculation], [Appraisal], [Cooking Daisukiyaki] (self-proclaimed)
● Hobbies: [Counting Coins], [Showing Affection on Beast-Person Triplets], [Cooking Daisukiyaki]
EPISODE 9 Alone
Re:ZERO
-Starting Life in Another World-
Truth of Zero

SUBARU...
...LET'S TALK.
WHY DID...
...YOU FIGHT WITH JULIUS?

I WANTED SOME PAYBACK.

HE SAID I WAS POWERLESS—UNWORTHY OF YOU...
...I HATED HIM FOR SAYING THAT AND DRIVING US APART.
THAT'S WHY.
...IS THAT ALL?
...ALL?
GU (CLENCH)

EMILIA, YOU JUST...
...DON'T GET IT.

—THAT'S RIGHT...

SHIT... I'M JUST...
...VENTING HERE...

SUBARU...

ROSWAAL AND I WILL BE RETURNING TO THE MANSION TOMORROW.
SUBARU, YOU WILL REMAIN HERE IN THE CAPITAL WITH LADY CRUSCH'S...
...HOUSE OF KARSTEN TO RECEIVE TREATMENT.

EH ...?

REM WILL REMAIN AS WELL, SO YOU'LL HAVE NOTHING TO WORRY ABOUT.
WAIT A SEC!
I HAVEN'T AGREED TO ANY OF THAT!
WHEN I'M HERE, YOU PUSH YOURSELF TOO HARD, DON'T YOU?

...WHEN WE FIRST MET... THEN AT THE MANSION...
BECAUSE I'M HERE, YOU—
I'M TELLING YOU TO WAIT!!
I...

I'VE JUST BEEN DOING WHATEVER I CAN FOR YOUR SAKE.
FOR... MY SAKE?
NO!

IT'S FOR YOUR SAKE, ISN'T IT?

BREAKING YOUR PROMISE, COMING TO THE CASTLE...
...FIGHTING JULIUS, EVEN USING MAGIC...
YOU'RE SAYING THAT WAS ALL FOR MY SAKE!?

I NEVER ONCE SAID...
GATA (RATTLE)
...I WANTED THAT!

I'M SORRY FOR BREAKING MY WORD...
I'M REALLY SORRY ABOUT THAT.
BUT NO! YOU'RE WRONG!
I'M NOT DOING THIS FOR ME...
IT'S FOR YOU...!

EMILIA... WON'T YOU TRUST ME?

I CAN'T.

YOU CAN'T UPHOLD A SINGLE PROMISE TO ME...
...SO I CAN'T DO THAT! ...I CAN'T...!

I WANT ...
...TO BELIEVE YOU...!

EMILIA ...

HEY, SUBARU ...

WHY DO YOU TRY TO HELP ME LIKE THAT?
—I SEE...

THIS IS WHAT'S BEEN TEARING HER UP INSIDE ...!
WHY DO I GO THAT FAR TO HELP HER...?
SHE DOESN'T KNOW WHY...
...BECAUSE I NEVER DID ANYTHING...
...TO PUT THOSE DOUBTS TO REST ...!!

—IT ALL STARTED WITH YOU.
YOU TRULY SAVED ME.
—EVEN IF YOU CAN'T REMEMBER THAT'S HOW WE MET...
...I WANT TO DO ALL I CAN FOR YOU...

...BECAUSE YOU SAVED ME.

I... SAVED YOU?
THAT'S RIGHT.

SUBARU... I DON'T UNDERSTAND ...

YOU CAN'T HELP WHAT YOU DON'T GET, BUT —!
—I TOLD YOU...
...I JUST DON'T GET IT!!

THE FIRST TIME WE MET WAS IN THE LOOT CELLAR, RIGHT?
WE NEVER MET BEFORE THAT!!

IF WE HAD, I'D—
I'D...
EMILIA!
LISTEN TO ME, EMILIA!!
IT'S THE TRUTH!!
WHEN I FIRST CAME TO THIS WORLD...

...YOU—
ZU
(BLOT)

OOOO
(WHOOOO)

—THE FROZEN WORLD...
FUWA (FLOAT)
IT WON'T LET ME REVEAL RETURN BY DEATH!!
GUOOO (GRAB)
GIRI (GRIND)
GIRI
GIRI
SH-SHIT ...!

FWOO...
SUBARU ...?

HFF!
HFF!
... AGAIN...
...YOU WON'T TELL ME ANY-THING...
GIRI (CLENCH)

WHAT SHOULD I DO...?
HOW DO I MAKE YOU UNDER-STAND!?
AT THE LOOT CELLAR, AT THE MANSION...
...IF I HADN'T BEEN THERE, IT WOULD'VE BEEN SO MUCH WORSE!!

NO ONE WOULD'VE BEEN SAVED!!
ISN'T THAT RIGHT!?

YOU HAVE TO OWE ME...
...AFTER ALL I'VE DONE FOR YOU—!!

THAT'S... TRUE.

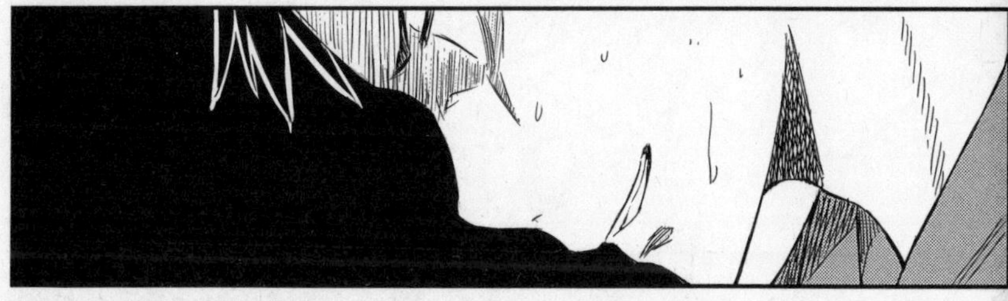

I DO OWE A REEEALLY BIG DEBT TO YOU, SUBARU, SO...

...I'LL REPAY IT ALL, THEN WE CAN END THIS.

REM WILL BE HERE SOON. DO AS SHE SAYS...
...I'LL ASK HER TO FOLLOW UP.

EMILIA...
HEY, SUBARU.
I'D... HOPED THAT...

...AT LEAST YOU...
...WOULDN'T GIVE ME SPECIAL TREATMENT...
...THAT YOU'D SEE ME AS JUST AN ORDINARY GIRL, ALL THE SAME...

I'M SORRY...
...SUBARU NATSUKI.
GIIII (CREAAAK)

BATAN (CLOSE)

I CAN'T...
...DO THAT ...

—AND SO, ON THIS DAY, FOR THE FIRST TIME...

...SUBARU NATSUKI WAS TRULY ALONE IN THAT OTHER WORLD.

—I'M SORRY ...
... SUBARU NATSUKI.
Episode 10 A Decaying-Mind
WAIT!!
I—
EMILIA!!
GABA (FLAP)

MORNING, HUH...?

IT HAS BEEN THREE DAYS SINCE SUBARU NATSUKI AND EMILIA PARTED WAYS...
...IN THE CAPITAL—
SUBARU NATSUKI IS BEING TREATED BY FERRIS AT THE CRUSCH KARSTEN RESIDENCE.

[FELT]

- One of the candidates for the next Queen of Lugunica.
- Originally a native of the slums of the Royal Capital of Lugunica turned light-fingered pickpocket.
- Subaru et al. knew her from the trouble over the badge but came to reunite with her at the royal selection conference.
- Blunt in personality and an opportunistic realist, she is like a stray cat, opening her heart only to those close to her.
- Sword Saint Reinhard discovered her as a candidate, but their relationship is rock-bottom. She attempted to flee to Old Man Rom, her only family, at every opportunity.
- Reinhard has spoken of her as someone with the potential for greatness, but that is currently a work in progress.
- Special skills: [Pickpocket], [Fleeing], [Milking Profits] (can tell whether an object is old or new)
- Hobbies: [Plotting to Escape the Slums] (currently on hold while she assembles a nest egg for doing so)

Episode 10

A Decaying Mind

Re:ZERO

-Starting Life in Another World-

Truth of Zero

SUBAWU, RELAX, RELAX!
MEW HAVE TO LET GO SO I CAN DO THE LAST TOUCHES, MEOW!
JI (STARE)
じー
RIGHT...

AH...
MEW GOT ALL STIFF AGAIN?
C'MEOWN... LET GO...
RELAX ...
RELAX ...

—LIKE...
...HELL I CAN—!!
HOW AM I SUPPOSED TO RELAX WHEN I HAVE A KITTY-EARED...
...PRETTY GIRL BREATHING DOWN MY NECK!?
PRETTY GIRL?
SUBAWU, MEW DON'T...?
YES, HE... PROBABLY DOES NOT KNOW...
WHA...?
I SAY SOMETHING WEIRD?
SUBARU...
MASTER FELIX IS, ER...

...MALE.
MEOW! ♥
A GUY—!?
MASTER FELIX'S GENDER IS RATHER FAMOUS IN THE CAPITAL.
FOR REAL...?
WANNA COME IN THE BATH AND CHECK?
NO WAY!!

WHY ARE PRECIOUS KITTY EARS ON SOMEONE SO...?
THAT MAKES IT BETTER!!
I DON'T SWING THAT WAY!!
YOUR HEART WAS AFLUTTER EARLIER...
SHADDAP!! FINISH UP ALREADY!!

MAN... THIS IS SUPPOSED TO BE HEALING ME, BUT I'M REALLY BEAT...
THAT CANNOT BE HELPED, SUBARU.
THE MOLD AND JUNK INSIDE YOUR BODY MUST BE FLUSHED OUT.
CAN'T YOU PUT THAT NICER?

HEY, REM.

WHAT IS IT...
SUBARU?

REM, DO YOU...
...THINK I'M PATHETIC?

I DO.
YOU DO!?

SO WHY DID YOU STAY WITH ME? ORDERS?

YOUR BEING PATHETIC MAKES ME WANT TO STAY WITH YOU.
I'M NOT BEING CONTRA-DICTORY EITHER.
REM IS HERE BECAUSE REM WANTS TO BE.
YOU REALLY ARE INCREDIBLE...
YES, BUT SISTER IS MORE SO.
CAN'T UNDER-STAND WHY YOU HAVE RAM ON THAT PEDESTAL ...

OKAY!
I'M A LITTLE PUMPED UP!
MIGHT AS WELL DO SOME, Y'KNOW, SWORD PRACTICE!
THAT SOUNDS GREAT!!
BORROW A WOODEN SWORD?
YES! I WANNA GIVE MY BODY A LI'L WORKOUT.
I SEE.
THEN I SHALL GLADLY LEND YOU ONE.
IN FACT, SUBARU NATSUKI...
...WHY NOT HAVE WILHELM INSTRUCT YOU WHILE YOU ARE AT IT?

MR... WILHELM?
IT HAS BEEN A WHILE...
...MR. SUBARU.
MY...
...YOU WERE ALREADY ACQUAINTED?
IT'S BEEN A WHILE!
WE MET AT ROSWAAL MANOR.
WILHELM VAN ASTREA
KARSTEN RESIDENCE SWORD INSTRUCTOR
IF YOU WISH, I SHALL BE YOUR SPARRING PARTNER.

PLEASE APPROACH ME AT FULL STRENGTH.
THAT WAY, I CAN ASSESS YOUR TRUE ABILITY.
COME ANY-TIME.
ALL RIGHT ...
HERE I COME!!
DA (RUN)

UNGH!!
KA (CLACK)
HMM...
KA
KAKA

TOO MUCH TENSION, MR. SUBARU. IN YOUR HANDS, FEET, NECK, HIPS...
...AND FACE...

MY FACE WAS ALWAYS LIKE THIS!

RAH!!

I KNOW FROM TRADING SWORDS WITH...

...MR. WILHELM IS...
...SUPER STRONG...!!

TON
(TAP)

GWEH!!
PAAN
(SNAP)

IDLE THOUGHTS SLIPPED INTO YOUR HEAD...
WHEN WIELDING A SWORD, THINK ONLY OF IT.

Y- YES, SIR...

HFF!
HFF!

NOW THEN, SHALL WE END IT HERE FOR TODAY...?

I'D... LOVE TO ASK FOR MORE, BUT I'VE HIT MY WALL.

MR. SUBARU, HOW ABOUT TOMORROW MORNING?
YOU FINE WITH THAT?
I HADN'T ASKED YET...
I DO NOT MIND.
SAME TIME TOMORROW, THEN.

IF YOU WILL EXCUSE ME, THE YOUNG LADY CAN HANDLE THE REST.
YES, SIR.
PEKORI (BOW)

TH-THANK YOU VERY MUCH!

WHAT IS IT, FERRIS?

RARE THAT GRANDPA WIL TAKES SUCH INTER-EST.

A TERRIBLE MISUNDER-STANDING.

THAT SO...?
NO WAY MEW'RE NOT INTERESTED IN PEOPLE...

THOUGH, MEW LIKE CUTTING THEM MORE THAN TALKING TO THEM.

...AN EVEN WORSE MISUNDER-STANDING.
THAT SO, MEOW?

MEW LIKE HIM THAT MUCH?
IS HE ACTUALLY TALENTED? FERRI DIDN'T NOTICE.
NOT SO MUCH.
HE IS AN AMATEUR WITH THE SWORD.

BUT THOSE EYES...
YES ...?

THAT BOY'S EYES ARE...
...THOSE OF ONE WHO HAS RETURNED FROM THE REALM OF DEATH.
INDEED, SEVERAL TIMES OVER...

MANY HAVE COME TO THE EDGE, STOPPED, AND TURNED BACK...
...BUT I KNOW OF NO OTHER WITH SUCH EYES.
HMMM.

FERRI DOESN'T REALLY GET IT...
SUBARU NATSUKI!!

NOW THEN, FERRIS, I MUST BE OFF...
'KAY...

SUBAWU PROBABLY ISN'T WALKING DOWN AN EASY ROAD...

AFTER ALL, HAVING THE SWORD DEVIL, WILHELM VAN ASTREA, TAKE A LIKING TO MEW...
...IS AS UNFORTUNATE AS THE WITCH HAVING A THING FOR MEW.

...I'M WEAK.

I SUPPOSE SO...
YOU SURE AGREED QUICKLY!!

PLEASE DO NOT MOVE SO MUCH...YOU WERE STRUCK ON THE HEAD.
I JUST... THOUGHT YOU MUST BE BORED.
IT'S ALL RIGHT.
I AM QUITE HAPPY ENOUGH.
HEY, REM...
WHAT IS IT, SUBARU?
WANNA GO BUY SOME ABBLES THIS MORNING?
THERE'S SOMEONE I OWE...
SOUNDS NICE! I WOULD LOVE TO GO.

SORRY TO DRAG YOU ALONG.
NOT AT ALL!
I LOOK FORWARD TO MEETING MASTER CADMON.
WATCH OUT—HIS FACE IS PRETTY HARD ON THE HEART.

WHOSE FACE IS HARD ON THE HEART!!?
CUT THAT OUT, YA PUNK ...!!

THERE IT IS—!!

POPS, DON'T GLARE AT CUSTOMERS WITH THAT FACE!!
SHUT UP, YOU TWO-TIMER!!

BROUGHT A DIFFERENT GIRL FROM LAST TIME, DIDN'T YOU!?
AH, I DON'T REMEMBER THE OTHER ONE MUCH, THOUGH.

I'M NOT SMOOTH ENOUGH TO TWO-TIME GIRLS.
ROZCHI'S SPECIAL ANTI-I.D. MANTLE SURE WORKS WONDERS...
THIS

BY THE WAY, THERE'RE A LOT OF PEOPLE TODAY. WHAT'S UP?

WELL, THAT'S 'COS THE ROYAL SELECTION STARTED UP.
TAKE A LOOK!

THEY PUT A HUGE SIGN OVER THERE...
RUMORS ABOUT IT ARE FLYING ALL OVER THE CITY.
OHH!

AND BIG EVENTS MEAN BIG CHANCES FOR PROFIT!
—NOT LIKE YOU'RE GETTING MUCH BUSINESS...
SHUT UP!!

—HEY, POPS, HOW DOES THE RACE LOOK TO YOU?
MM?

LET'S SEE...
OF THE FIVE CANDIDATES, THE NAMES I KNOW ARE...
...DUCHESS CRUSCH KARSTEN AND THE HOSHIN COMPANY PRESIDENT, ANASTASIA.
GAYA (CHATTER)
GAYA
KUI (TURN)
LADY CRUSCH INHERITED THE TITLE OF DUCHESS AT A YOUNG AGE.
THEY SAY SHE HAS A RARE GENIUS, EVEN IN ALL THE KINGDOM'S HISTORY.
EVERY BUSINESSMAN KNOWS HOW THE HOSHIN COMPANY'S EXPLODED IN A FEW YEARS.
SECOND COMING OF "HOSHIN OF THE WASTES," THEY SAY.

ANYWAY, RUMOR HAS IT THOSE TWO ARE THE FAVORITES.
COMPARED TO THEM, THE OTHER THREE ARE UNKNOWNS.
BARELY ANYONE HERE'S EVEN HEARD THE NAMES.
BUT...
...HAVING A HALF-ELF CANDIDATE? I THINK THEY'VE LOST THEIR MINDS!
HAVING A HALF-DEMON BECOME QUEEN AIN'T NO JOKE...
...WHAT THE HELL ARE THE HIGHER-UPS THINKING...?
MM? WHAT? WENT ALL QUIET THERE.
I THINK YOU'RE... A GOOD GUY, POPS...
... SO LET ME SAY THIS.

DON'T SELL HER SHORT JUST 'COS SHE'S A HALF-ELF!
I DUNNO ABOUT THE WITCH OF JEALOUSY, BUT...
...WHAT'S SHE EVER DONE TO YOU?
I DO NOT KNOW IF MY EFFORTS ARE WORTHY OF THE THRONE...
...BUT NONE OF THE OTHER CANDIDATES' FEELINGS RUN DEEPER THAN MINE!

MAYBE SHE'S AMAZING... MAYBE SHE'S THINKING ABOUT THIS COUNTRY'S WELL-BEING...
SHE MIGHT BE INCREDIBLE, FOR ALL YOU KNOW!
SO...

...LOOK AT HER FAIRLY!
HER NAME'S EMILIA!
NO FAMILY NAME! JUST EMILIA!

ALL RIGHT, ALL RIGHT.
SORRY I WENT TOO FAR...

BUT WHATEVER YOU THINK...
...THE WITCH IS TERROR ITSELF TO MOST PEOPLE ...

...AND THAT WON'T CHANGE!

SO, IF YOU'RE NOT BUYIN' ANYTHIN', YOU'RE IN THE WAY.
I'M BUYING.
HOW 'BOUT TEN ABBLES? I MEANT TO BUY TWENTY, BUT...
NWHA!?
HEY, SUBARU...

...I'D HOPED THAT...AT LEAST YOU WOULDN'T...
...GIVE ME SPECIAL TREATMENT...

SHIT...
EMILIA...!

HYOOOOO
(CHILL)

MY BRAIN...
...TREMBLES...

AHH...
BOKI (SNAP)
BOKI
BOKI

YOU...
...ARE SLOTH-FUL, YES ...?
to be continued...

Illustration by Shinichirou Otsuka (Character Designer)

Re:ZERO -Starting Life in Another World-

Supporting Comments from the Author of the Original Work, Tappei Nagatsuki

Daichi Matsuse-sensei, congratulations on the release of Volume 2!
This line has already become a cliché, but thank you for your latest efforts for *Re:ZERO*!
With the number of characters growing exponentially in Chapter 3, your touches in drawing the royal candidates, knights, and so forth, as well as your creative flourishes, were all very entertaining.
In particular, the trying scenes that greatly moved the characters emotionally in this volume became even more trying! The fun scenes were even more fun! I went from unusually and highly satisfied to extremely satisfied!
I'm getting more impressions from readers saying, "With the anime about to air, I'm gonna read the comic to learn about the original!" I'm sure we'll both be making *Re:ZERO* even more popular from here on out!
With *Re:ZERO*'s third chapter revving up in earnest, do enjoy the Matsuse version of *Re:ZERO*!

AFTERWORD

HELLO, MATSUSE HERE.
THANK YOU VERY MUCH FOR PURCHASING CHAPTER 3, VOLUME 2.
AROUND THE TIME I WAS DRAWING EPISODE 10, I STRAINED MY BACK, BUT I SOMEHOW MANAGED TO OVERCOME IT. I'D BETTER GET SOME PROPER EXERCISE...
NOW, THEN. FINALLY, THE LONG-AWAITED ANIME HAS ARRIVED!! I THINK IT'S A TON OF FUN SEEING SUBARU AND EMILIA MOVE AND SPEAK. I WANT TO MAKE THE COMIC EVERY BIT AS STIRRING!
INCIDENTALLY, ON A PERSONAL LEVEL, THE SCENE IN THIS VOLUME WITH REINHARD BOWING BEFORE FELT WAS MY FAVORITE IN THE SERIES TO DATE.
I PUT THEM ON THE FRONT COVER THIS TIME AROUND BECAUSE I REALLY LIKE THAT PAIRING.
LAST BUT NOT LEAST, TO ALL READERS, YOUR VOICES HAVE TRULY SUPPORTED ME.
AS ALWAYS, THANK YOU VERY MUCH.
WELL THEN, SEE YOU NEXT TIME!!

Re:ZERO -Starting Life in Another World-

Artist Comments

Death doesn't stop a video game–loving shut-in from going on adventures and fighting monsters!

KONOSUBA: GOD'S BLESSING ON THIS WONDERFUL WORLD!

SOUL EATER

THE COMPLETE SERIES AVAILABLE NOW!

(25 VOLUMES IN ALL!)

Yen
Press

SOUL EATER
NOT!

RE:ZERO -STARTING LIFE IN ANOTHER WORLD- 2
Chapter 3: Truth of Zero

Art: Daichi Matsuse
Original Story: Tappei Nagatsuki
Character Design: Shinichirou Otsuka

Translation: ZephyrRZ
Lettering: Anthony Quintessenza

Yen Press
1290 Avenue of the Americas
New York, NY 10104

Visit us at yenpress.com
facebook.com/yenpress
twitter.com/yenpress
yenpress.tumblr.com
instagram.com/yenpress

First Yen Press Edition: January 2018

Yen Press is an imprint of Yen Press, LLC.
The Yen Press name and logo are trademarks of Yen Press, LLC.

The publisher is not responsible for websites (or their content) that are not owned by the publisher.

Library of Congress Control Number: 2016936537

ISBNs: 978-0-316-55948-5 (paperback)
978-0-316-55950-8 (ebook)

10 9 8 7 6 5 4 3 2 1

BVG

Printed in the United States of America